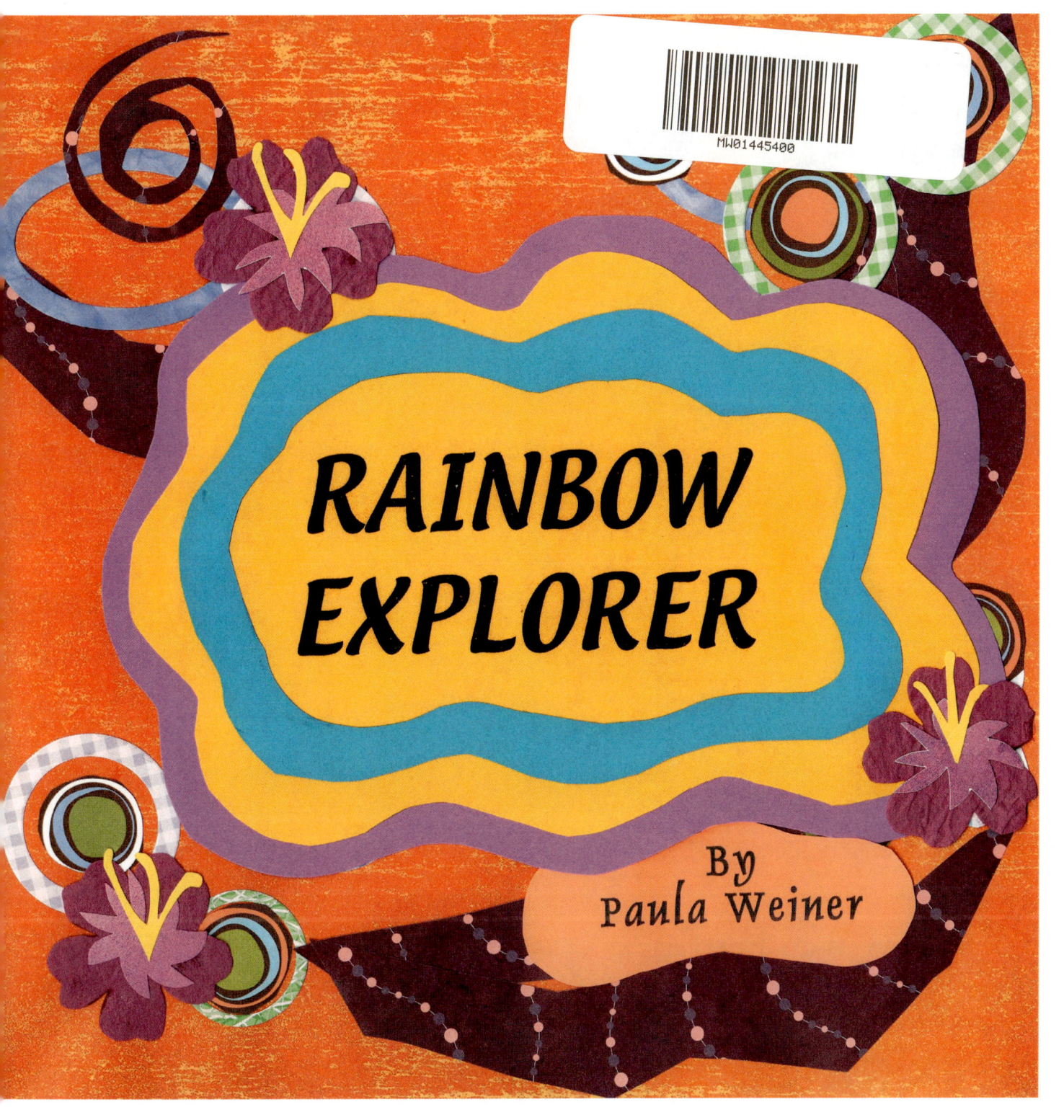

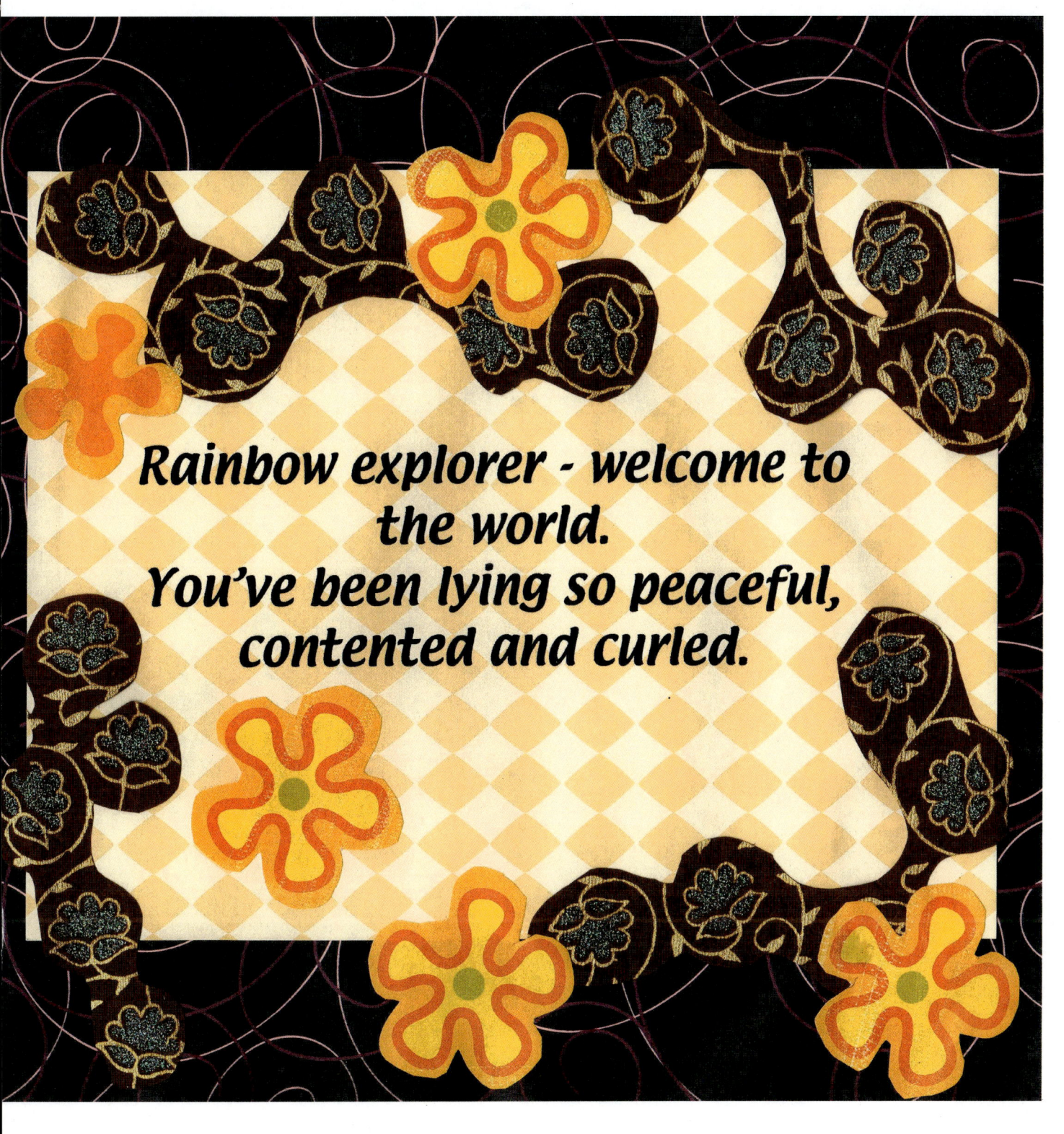

Gear up for this sizzling, ear popping ride.
Jump aboard, get the first car, no need to hide.

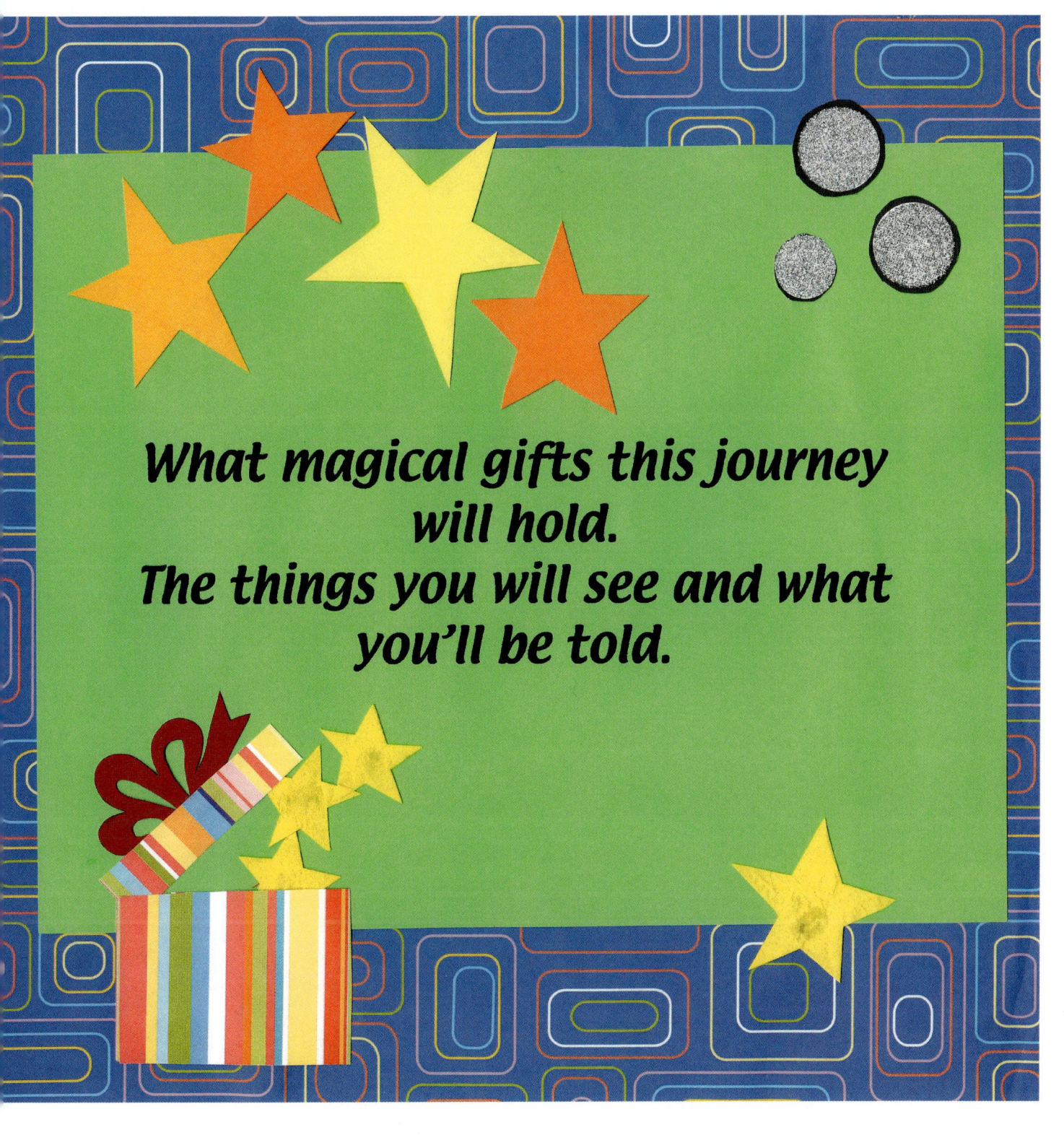

What magical gifts this journey will hold.
The things you will see and what you'll be told.

Splash in puddles simply because they are there.
Let the wind toss your kite and mess up your hair.

When you see something alluring get out, look around.
After all your feet are not plastered to ground.

Head for the beach, squishing sand in your toes.
Dance with the ocean as waves ebb and flow.

Stand silent and awestruck as the golden sun dips.
As beyond the horizon new days will lift.

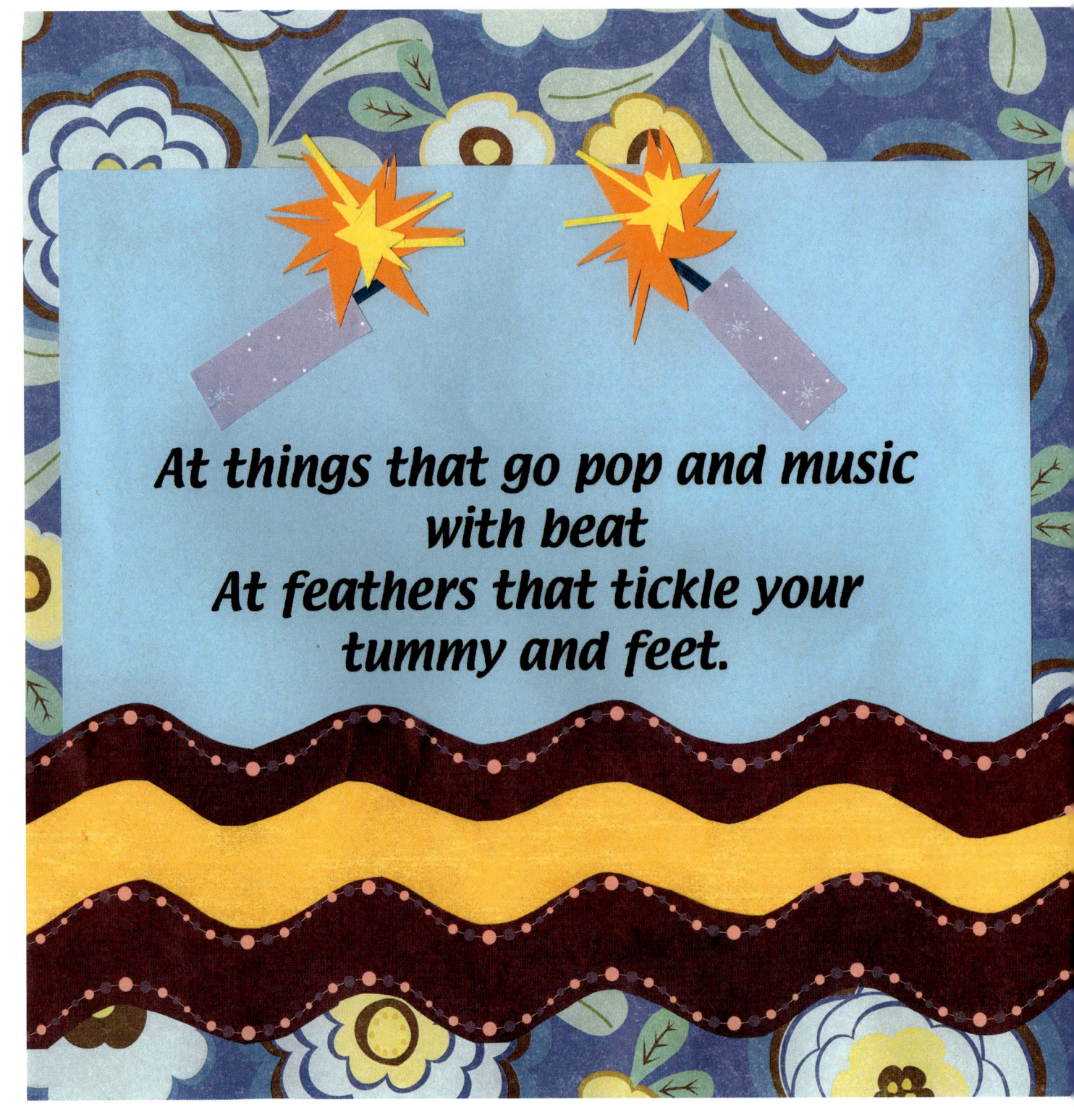

At things that go pop and music with beat
At feathers that tickle your tummy and feet.

You'll be flooded with advice on just how to live.
Some will push, others pull, some take and some give.

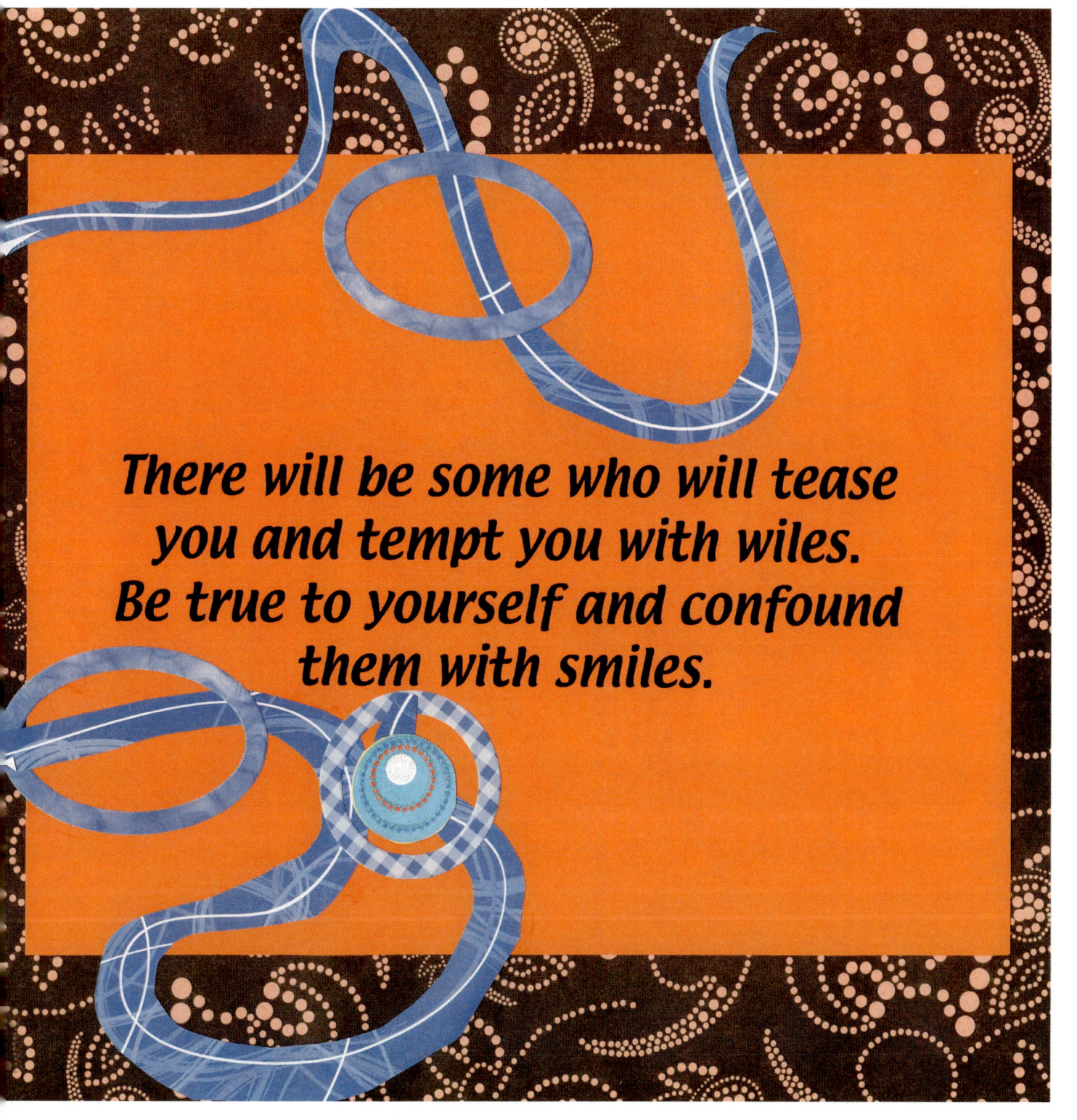

There will be some who will tease you and tempt you with wiles.
Be true to yourself and confound them with smiles.

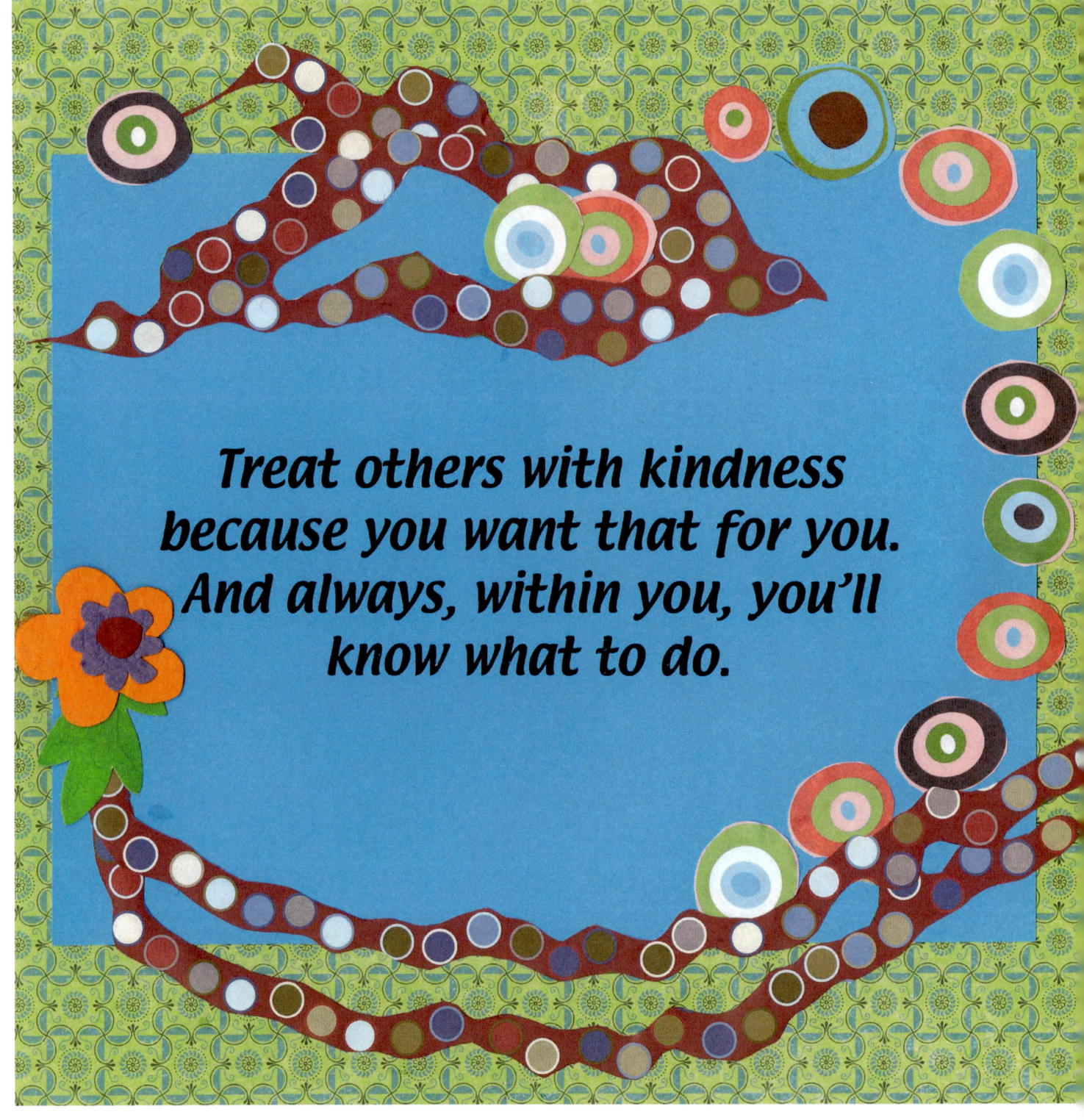

Treat others with kindness because you want that for you. And always, within you, you'll know what to do.

We'll surround you with love and act as your guide
In this wild, serendipitous, thrill seeking ride.

Made in the USA
Monee, IL
29 March 2021